Yash and Yashika Learn about Coding

Story cum activity book on coding for young children

SCHOLASTIC
New York Toronto London Auckland
Sydney New Delhi Hong Kong

Published by Scholastic India Pvt. Ltd.
A subsidiary of Scholastic Inc., New York, 10012 (USA).
Publishers since 1920, with international operations in Canada,
Australia, New Zealand, the United Kingdom, India, and Hong Kong.

For information regarding permission, write to:
Scholastic India Pvt. Ltd.
A-27, Ground Floor, Sigma Centre
Infocity-1, Sector 34, Gurgaon-122001 (India)

First edition: July 2020
This reprint edition: February 2023

ISBN-13: 978-93-9006-678-0

E-book ISBN-13: 978-93-9006-662-9

Printed in India at Saurabh Printers Pvt. Ltd.

Story and concept: Dr. Swati Popat Vats
Activities: Dimple Shah, Manasi Bist & Nisha Thakkar
Design: Pranali Shinde

Dear Parent and Educator,

You must be wondering why a coding book for young children?

Steve Jobs said, 'Everyone should learn how to code, it teaches you to think.' We expose children to technology and screens without understanding its all round impact. Robots have made their appearance around us, be it Siri, Google Home, Alexa or the Internet of toys etc. Children cannot understand how these machines talk, move, remember and do things. It is time to teach children that the technology that they see around them is not magic but is created by us—Humans. It's time to educate the 'digital natives' about computational thinking and technology literacy (I have used this term to encompass all kinds of tech, digital and screen usage).

In the foundational years of life and education (2 to 10 years), we need to understand children's need for play and tinkering and how this can be connected to later computational thinking skills. Jean Piaget, a Swiss psychologist, defined schemas of play. Schemas are described as patterns of repeated behaviour which allow children to explore and express developing ideas and thoughts through play.

The 9 schemas of play are:

1. Orientation: the urge to hang upside down; to see things from a different point of view.

2. Positioning: lining up things neatly.

3. Connections: trying to understand the connection between whole and parts, and parts and whole.

4. Trajectory: throwing things to understand how things move and the relationship between speed, throw and objects.

5. Enclosure: container; to try to understand how things fit into spaces.

6. Transporting: carrying things from one place to another using different methods.

7. Enveloping: covering things and themselves, hiding.

8. Rotation: enjoying the sensation of going round and round. Rotating things and objects.

9. Transformation: mixing things, seeing how they change, how they react and how it feels.

These 9 schemas are what we call 'tinkering' and coding requires all of them. So in children's play is hidden the knowledge of coding! When children are TINKERING, they are changing things to see what happens; when they are CREATING, they are designing and making; when they are finding and fixing errors in block play or worksheets they are DEBUGGING; when they keep going in spite of mistakes they are PERSEVERING; in group play they are COLLABORATING, working together. They are using LOGIC when they are predicting and analysing during story time, and during sand and water play, they are EVALUATING, making judgements. When we teach them the steps of a task or rules to follow, we are teaching them about ALGORITHMS. They see PATTERNS and are able to spot similarities. When they cannot understand complex tasks like toilet training or brushing their teeth, we help them break it down into steps and we teach them DECOMPOSITION. And when we are teaching them manners, we are actually teaching them about CONDITIONALS (IF-THEN)—what would happen if ... if I am angry and hit someone, or if I am eating, then I should not speak, etc. When you help children sort their toys and books and crayons, that is VARIABLES AND ARRAYS in code language!

Children are born explorers. They question, tinker, think, create ... all the skills required to be a good coder. This book helps parents understand how coding activities like algorithm, decompose, conditionals, variables etc. are already a part of everyday play and daily activities.

Computational thinking is formulating problems in a way that enables us to use a computer and other tools to help solve them. It means logically organizing and analysing data. Teaching children computational thinking means teaching children **'what to do with data'** instead of **'just collecting data!'** This means teaching young brains **'how to learn'** and not just **'what to learn!'**

'All our children deserve a chance to become creators instead of consumers of computer science' Maria Klawe

Coding develops computational thinking and computational thinking is nothing but learning to relate, apply and understand.

Here are some coding terms and their connection to everyday learning activities of young children.

1. Coding – is a set of instructions

Listen and follow instructions

- To learn to code effectively and efficiently, you need to learn to follow instructions correctly in order to solve problems and reach your goal.
- Listening and following directions are important skills that span several areas of child development.

2. Algorithm – is a sequence of codes

- Sequencing is understanding how a series of objects or events occur in a specific and logical order.
- Sequencing activities help to improve logical understanding and reasoning skills in children. Sequencing is one of the most important skills needed to learn to code. Children sequence during block play, singing rhymes or following a routine/timetable.

Sequencing requires two skills—sorting and patterning

a. Sorting

- This is the process or operation of ordering items and data according to specific criteria.
- Sorting and classifying objects helps children begin to notice how items are alike and different, and creates an awareness that is important in learning to code. Sorting objects, colours and shapes are all activities that children do every day.

b. Patterning:

- Encouraging a child's understanding of patterns contributes to the development of various kinds of mathematical thinking, including counting and problem-solving.
- Patterning activities provides a sense of order in what might otherwise appear chaotic and helps to see relationships. It helps children understand, 'what comes before', 'what comes after' and helps them see the continuity in stories, rhymes and everyday activities.

3. Decomposition – in coding when you decompose a problem or a task, you break it down into smaller tasks.

- When we give instructions to children in steps or when we help them break a task down into steps or when we divide the food on their plate into manageable chunks, we are decomposing a problem or a task!

4. Debugging – is when you go looking for bugs and errors in your program and fix it to achieve the desired output.

- Activities that help children find out what is missing, or the odd one out, is helping them develop debugging skills!

5. If-then-else conditionals – helps the program to perform a certain action when faced with choices.

- What would happen if: 'If I want to colour a picture, then I need crayons,' or 'If I want to observe a plant grow, then I need to sow a seed' etc. these are all everyday **If-Then conditionals** that we already expose our children to.

6. Looping – is a set of instructions in a program or algorithm that are repeated again and again.

- When you add a loop in a sequence you are programming the machine to repeat certain steps to reach the desired output.
- Many nursery rhymes and stories have loops! Like 'Five little ducks went out one day …' or the story of 'Goldilocks', in both of them the same thing is repeated again and again. These are loops that children are already experiencing in their daily learning activities.

How to use this storivity book

Tell the story and then do the activities with your child or tell the story and do the activities as they appear in the book. Some children will want to first hear the full story before doing the activities and some will want to do the activity to understand what the characters are doing. So choose the style that best suits your child.

Introduction to the characters in the story

This is Yash.

He loves reading books, taking their dog Bruno for walks in the park and he is often found learning about computers or playing with his twin Yashika.

This is Yashika.

She loves to play football, play piano and solve puzzles. She loves to learn how things work and is often found helping her dad fix stuff around the house.

This Yash and Yashika's mother.

She is a coder by profession. She works in a technology firm. She loves gardening and working on activity books and puzzles with Yash and Yashika.

This is Yash and Yashika's father.

He is a chef. He is often found trying new recipes and reading different books. He is also seen fixing things around the house with his daughter Yashika.

This is Mr. Bot.

He is a robot. He was built by Yash and Yashika's mom. He loves to go on coding quests with Yash and Yashika. The children also use him to help them in their chores. Their mother has taught them how to program him.

X
Y
Z

Yash and Yashika's mother introduced them to the dancing robot, Mr. Bot. They enjoyed watching Mr. Bot sing, dance, kick a ball and tell stories. They thought that Mr. Bot was a magical creature! Their mother explained to them that Mr. Bot did not have any magic, he was a robot and he had a computer inside him.

Yashika asked, ‘But, then how does he know how to kick a ball? I have a computer too but it does not kick a ball.’

‘Well,’ said Mother, ‘if I give your computer hands, legs and a face, it will become a robot. And then we can make it do things too.’

X
Y
Z

Yash asked curiously, ‘Does Mr. Bot speak like us?’

‘Yes,’ said Mother, ‘we can train it to speak in any language.’

‘What else can it do?’ asked Yashika.

‘Mr. Bot can do whatever we teach him to do. Do you want to teach Mr. Bot to run fast?’ asked Mother.

‘Yes, we do!’ said Yash and Yashika.

Stand up.
Walk to your cupboard.
Open your cupboard.
Take out your raincoat.
Wear your raincoat.
Close the cupboard.
Walk to the door.
Wear your rain boots.
Wait for Mummy.

'For Mr. Bot to do anything, he first needs to be given instructions,' said Mother. 'For example, when I take you to school when its raining, I ask you to ...'

Stand up.

↓

Walk to your cupboard.

↓

Open your cupboard.

↓

Take out your raincoat.

↓

Wear your raincoat.

↓

Close the cupboard.

↓

Walk to the door.

↓

Wear your rain boots.

↓

Wait for Mummy.

'Right?' asked Mother.

If we give less instructions, it confuses Mr. Bot!

Stand up

↓

Arrange the books

↓

Stop

We need to give step-by-step instructions in a sequence to Mr. Bot.

Stand up

↓

Move five steps towards the book

↓

Pick up the book

↓

Turn left

↓

Move seven steps towards the book shelf

↓

Keep the book on the book shelf

↓

Stop

‘Just like that, Mr. Bot needs to be told the steps in his language and his language is called a code. He needs to be told everything in the right order (sequence) or he will not be able to understand and will get confused.’

‘So who puts this code into him?’ asked Yashika.

‘People who code computers are called computer programmers and they code gadgets and robots like Mr. Bot,’ replied Mother.

Mother gave Yash and Yashika some sequencing activities to do.

Sequencing

This is your jumbled up going-to-bed routine. Put it in the correct sequence.

Going to bed

Well done! You can sequence now.

Sequencing

This is your getting-ready-for-school routine, but jumbled up. Put it in the correct sequence.

Getting ready for school.

Well done! You can sequence! You are now ready for other coding activities.

Sequencing

Rhymes have a sequence too!

The sequence of the given rhyme is jumbled up. Write the correct sequence in the boxes below.

Read and enjoy the rhyme

One, two,
Buckle my shoe;
Three, four,
Shut the door;
Five, six,
Pick up sticks;
Seven, eight,
Lay them straight;
Nine, ten,
A big fat hen!

Five, six, Pick up sticks;

Nine, ten, A big fat hen!

One, two, Buckle my shoe;

Three, four, Shut the door;

Seven, eight, Lay them straight;

Write the correct sequence here: ☐ ☐ ☐ ☐ ☐

Well done! You can now put rhymes in the correct sequence.

Sequencing

Try this rhyme too.

The sequence of the given rhyme is jumbled up. Write the correct sequence in the boxes below.

Read and enjoy the rhyme

Where is Thumbkin? Where is Thumbkin?
Here I am! Here I am!
How are you this morning?
Very well, I thank you.
Run away. Run away.

Where is Pointer?Where is Pointer?
Here I am! Here I am!
How are you this morning?
Very well, I thank you.
Run away. Run away.

Where is Middleman? Where is Middleman?
Here I am! Here I am!
How are you this morning?
Very well, I thank you.
Run away. Run away.

Where is Ringman? Where is Ringman?
Here I am! Here I am!
How are you this morning?
Very well, I thank you.
Run away. Run away.

Where is Pinkie? Where is Pinkie?
Here I am! Here I am!
How are you this morning?
Very well, I thank you.
Run away. Run away.

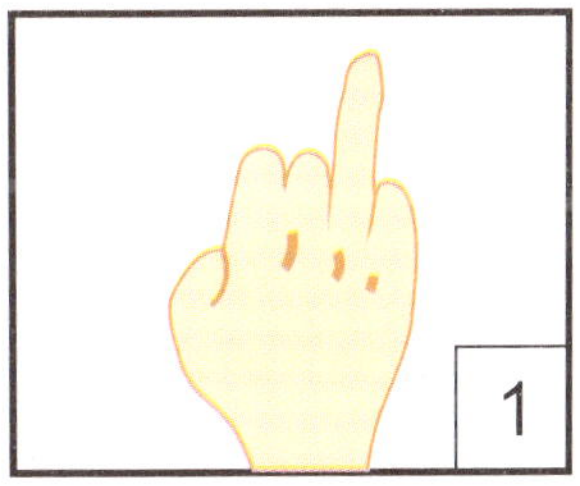

Where is Ringman? Where is Ringman?
Here I am! Here I am!
How are you this morning?
Very well, I thank you.
Run away. Run away.

Where is Middleman? Where is Middleman?
Here I am! Here I am!
How are you this morning?
Very well, I thank you.
Run away. Run away.

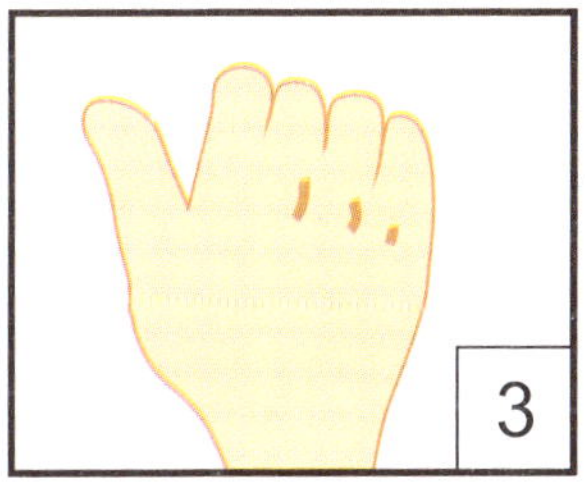

Where is Thumbkin? Where is Thumbkin?
Here I am! Here I am!
How are you this morning?
Very well, I thank you.
Run away. Run away.

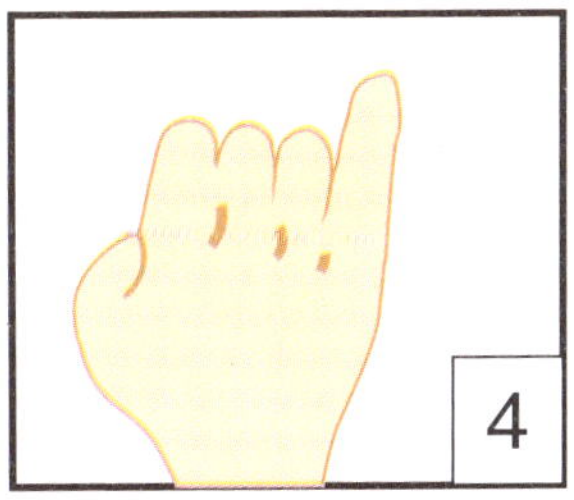

Where is Pinkie? Where is Pinkie?
Here I am! Here I am!
How are you this morning?
Very well, I thank you.
Run away. Run away.

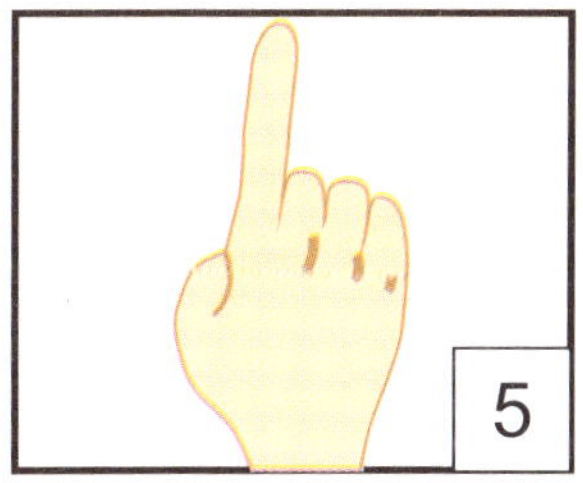

Where is Pointer? Where is Pointer?
Here I am! Here I am!
How are you this morning?
Very well, I thank you.
Run away. Run away.

Write the correct sequence here: ☐ ☐ ☐ ☐ ☐

You are a sequencing star!

Algorithm for Mr. Bot

Soon it was snack time and Mother said, 'Mr. Bot will make sandwiches for all of us. Let us tell him the steps.'

The children told Mr. Bot the steps and he made the perfect sandwich.

'Great,' said Mother, 'you have made an algorithm for Mr. Bot to follow. A set of steps or codes is called an algorithm and robots follow an algorithm, like you follow a timetable or a routine.'

'Now here are some algorithm activities for you,' said Mother. 'Let's see if you can solve them.'

Algorithm

Choose and place the correct arrows in the grid to make the monkey reach the bananas.

↓	→	←	↑

Draw the correct algorithm here:

Well done! You are beginning to learn about algorithms.

Algorithm

Look at these algorithm sets. Which one will you use to help the mouse reach the cheese? Tick the correct set and draw the arrows in the grid below.

Algorithm set 1	Algorithm set 2
↓ ↓ →	↓ ↓ ↓ ←

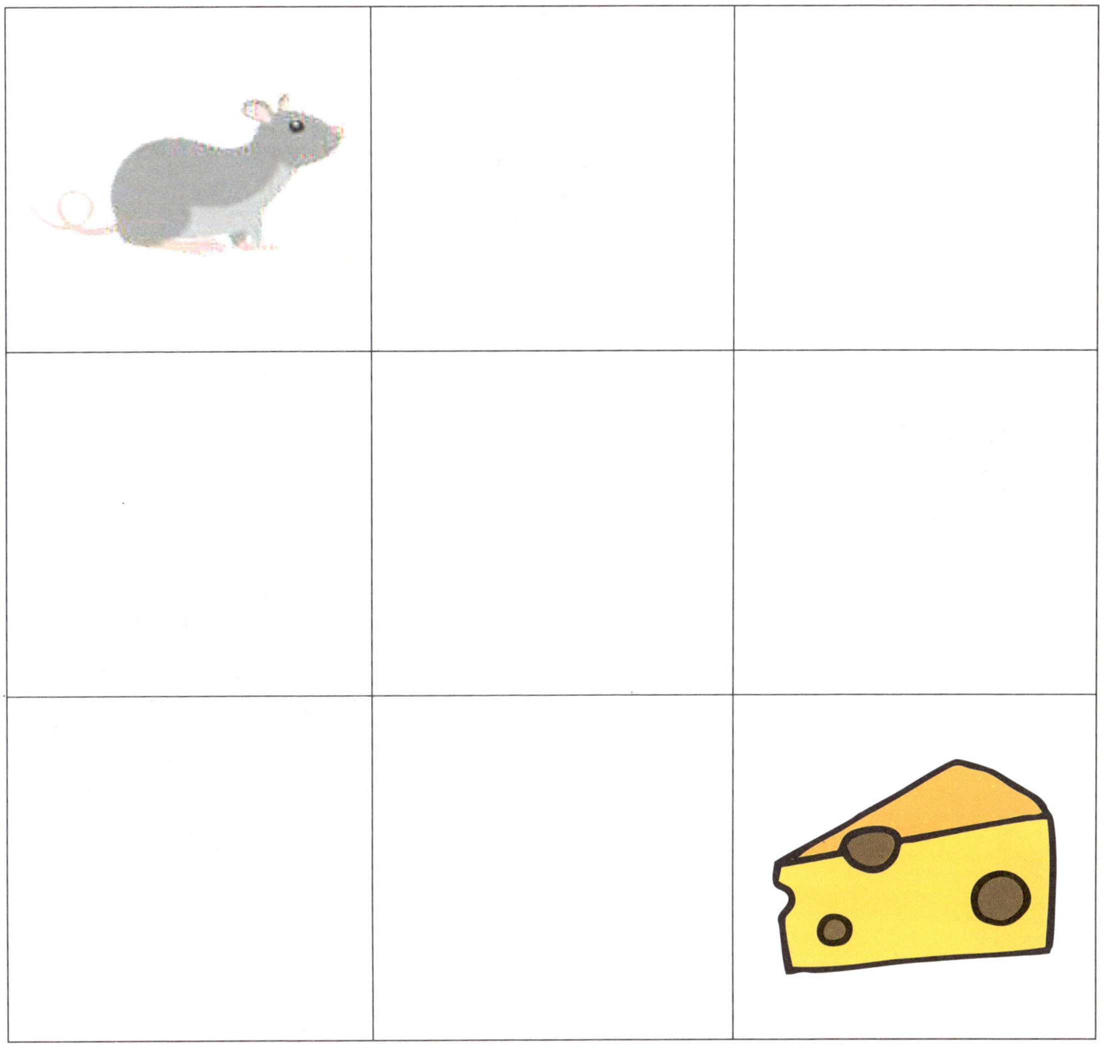

You have now understood algorithms. Well done!

Five little ducks went out one day,
over the hill and far away.
Mother duck said, "Quack, quack, quack."
But only four little ducks came back, back, back.
Four little ducks went out one day,
over the hill and far away.
Mother duck said, "Quack, quack, quack."
But only three little ducks came back, back, back.
Three little ducks went out one day,
over the hill and far away.
Mother duck said, "Quack, quack, quack."
But only two little ducks came back, back, back.
Two little ducks went out one day,
over the hill and far away.
Mother duck said, "Quack, quack, quack"
But only one little duck came back, back, back.
One little duck went out one day,
over the hill and far away.
Mother duck said, "Quack, quack, quack."
But none of the little ducks came back, back, back.

Yash and Yashika sang their favourite rhyme ‘Five little ducks’ for Mr. Bot. ‘Children, did you notice that some lines are being repeated in the song?’ asked their mother. She showed them the song on a chart. It looked like this.

‘The whole song is the same, only the number changes in every stanza, this means that the same stanza is repeated again and again. And that is called a loop,’ explained Mother.

Looping

The song 'Five little ducks' uses a loop with a different number of ducks each time. Sing the song and colour off a duck each time you go round the loop. The first one has been coloured for you.

Good job! You now understand loops.

Five little ducks went out one day,
over the hill and far away.
Mother duck said, 'Quack, quack, quack.'
But only four little ducks came back, back, back.

Four little ducks went out one day,
over the hill and far away.
Mother duck said, 'Quack, quack, quack.'
But only three little ducks came back, back, back.

Three little ducks went out one day,
over the hill and far away.
Mother duck said, 'Quack, quack, quack.'
But only two little ducks came back, back, back.

Two little ducks went out one day,
over the hill and far away.
Mother duck said, 'Quack, quack, quack'
But only one little duck came back, back, back.

One little duck went out one day,
over the hill and far away.
Mother duck said, 'Quack, quack, quack.'
But none of the little ducks came back, back, back.

After eating their sandwiches, the children were looking forward to playing more with Mr. Bot.

Mother said, ‘Now, we will give instructions to Mr. Bot to complete an obstacle course. We will set up the obstacle course and then guide Mr. Bot on what to do when he faces the obstacle.’

The children quickly put some blocks, books and hoopla rings on the floor as obstacles for Mr. Bot. Mother switched on Mr. Bot and he started walking. But he stopped at the first obstacle of books.

‘So children, what do you think Mr. Bot should do now?’ asked Mother.

‘He should walk around or jump over the pile of books,’ said Yashika.

‘Yes,’ said their mother. ‘If there is space then he can walk around, if not, he can jump. So let us now create an if-then instruction for Mr. Bot.’

Yashika gave Mr. Bot an if-then condition. She said, ‘Mr. Bot, if there is an obstacle then walk around or jump over it. If there is no obstacle then walk straight.’

Mr. Bot followed the instructions correctly and the children cheered for him. Yash and Yashika were now excited to play more if-then games designed by their mother.

If-Then conditionals

Here is a simple 'If-Then' activity for you.

If 1  , then jump

If 2 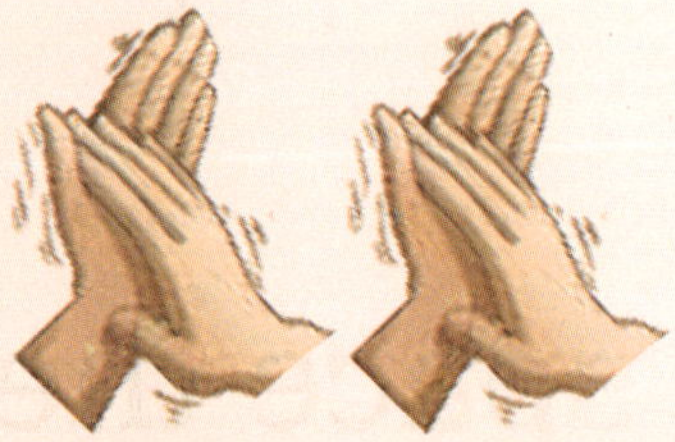 , then turn around

If 3  , then fly like a bird

If 4 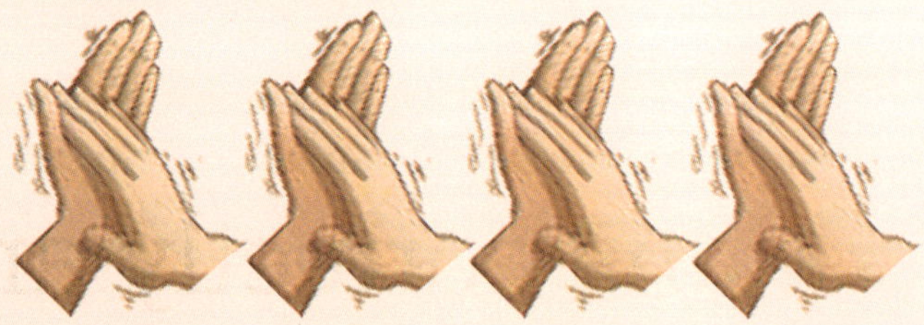 , then hop like a frog

Good job! You are beginning to understand If-Then conditionals.

If-Then-Else

Let's play this 'If-Then' game. Roll a dice. Count the number on the dice. Move that many steps on the path given below. If it is an animal, then you can roll the dice again, else/if not then wait for your next turn.

Wonderful! You can now play If-Then-Else games.

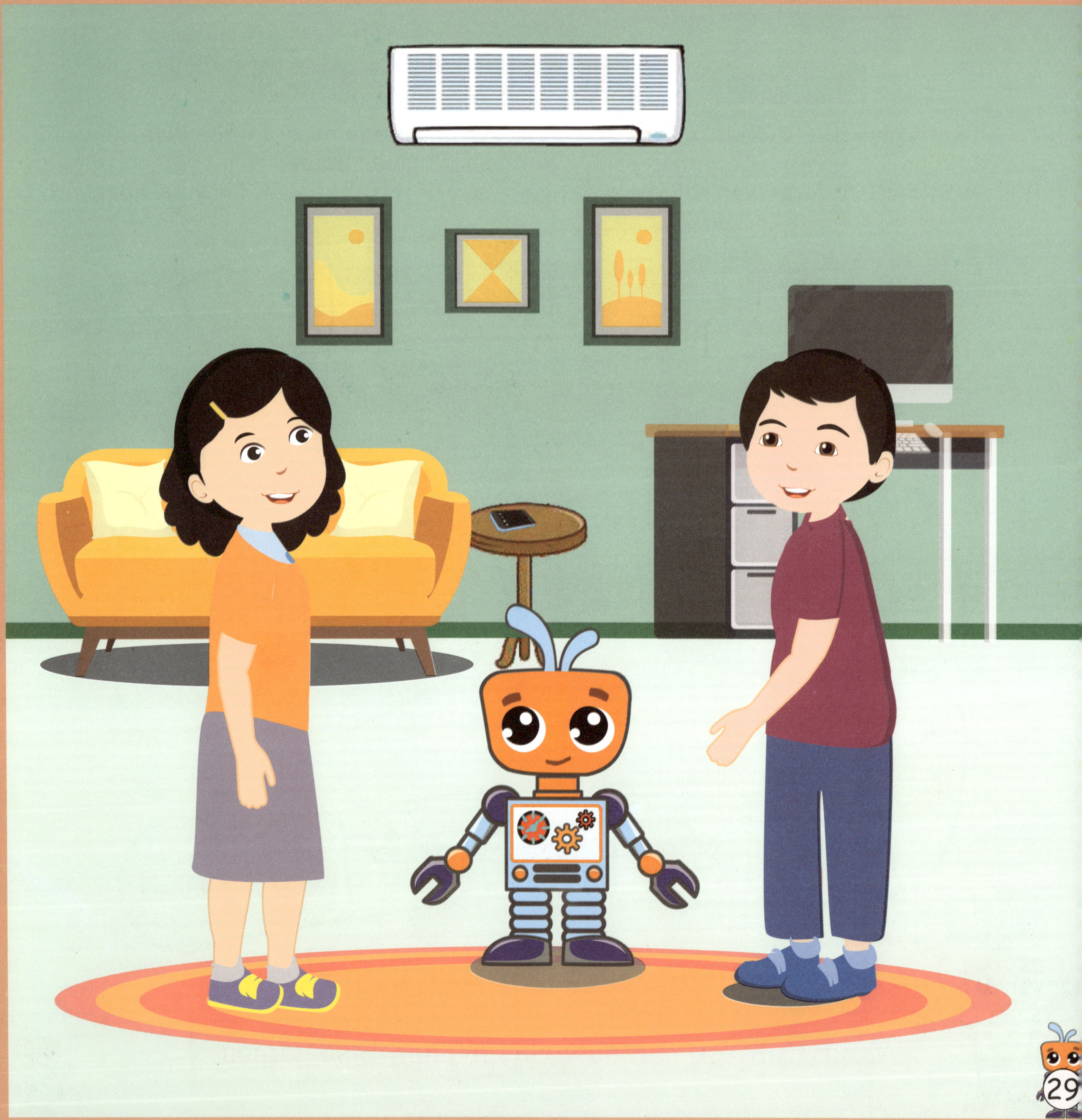

Yashika and Yash were very excited to learn that Mr. Bot codes, loops, follows if-then conditions and much more.

'If a gadget can do something on its own, it means there is a computer in it,' said Mother. Yash and Yashika went around the house identifying and naming all the gadgets that have a computer in them.

Join Yash and Yashika on a digital hunt

The following 7 devices are hidden in Yash and Yashika's home. Find and circle them.

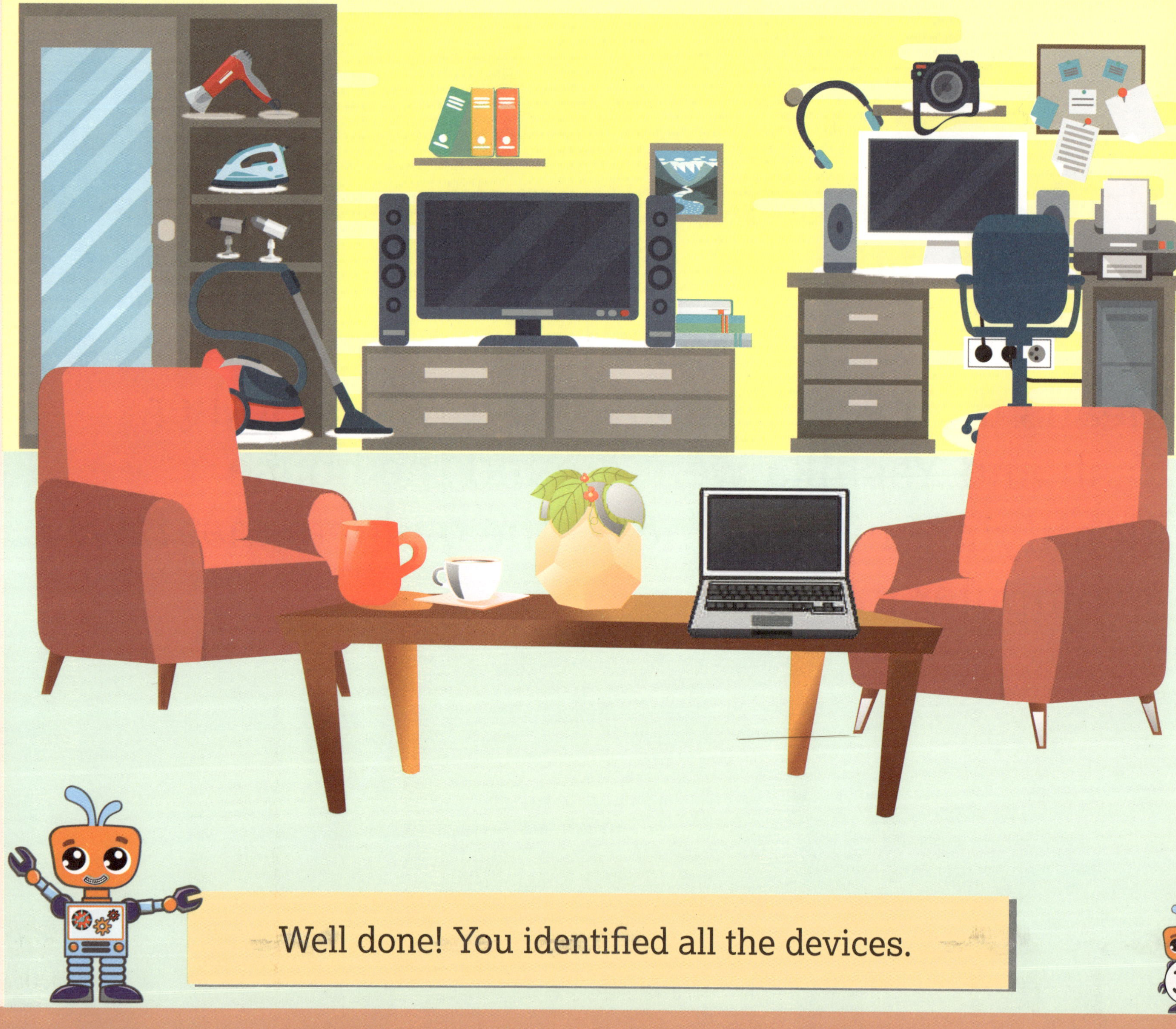

Well done! You identified all the devices.

Story
Treasure

It was now time for bed and both Yash and Yashika were happy as bedtime meant story and lullaby time.

Today, it was their father's turn to tell them a story. They opened the storybook and asked their father to read the story of Red Riding Hood.

But the story was jumbled up with pages from Goldilocks and Hansel and Gretel in between.

‘Oh dear,’ said their father. ‘Looks like the pages are mixed up. We have to debug the book!’

Yash and Yashika peered at the pages trying to find the bugs. ‘Where are the bugs?’ asked Yash.

Their father smiled and said that when a robot makes an error it is said that there is a ‘bug’ in its code! So they happily found all the bugs (errors) and put the pages of the storybook in the right order.

Let's try a debugging activity

Circle the obstacle that made Jack and Jill fall down the hill.

Well done! You identified all the bugs!

ON
OFF

Yash and Yashika now knew that there were many computers around them and that computers needed us to tell them what to do. They were not magical!

As she drifted off to sleep, Yashika told her father she wanted to be a coder when she grows up! And Yash wanted to make a robot that flies!

Answer key

Sequencing

This is your jumbled up going-to-bed routine. Put it in the correct sequence.

Going to bed

6

5

4

2

1

3

Sequencing

This is your getting-ready-for-school routine, but jumbled up. Put it in the correct sequence.

Getting ready for school.

1

6

2

5

4

7

3

Sequencing

Rhymes have a sequence too!
The sequence of the given rhyme is jumbled up. Write the correct sequence in the boxes below.

Read and enjoy the rhyme

One, two,
Buckle my shoe;
Three, four,
Shut the door;
Five, six,
Pick up sticks;
Seven, eight,
Lay them straight;
Nine, ten,
A big fat hen!

Five, six, Pick up sticks;

Nine, ten, A big fat hen!

One, two, Buckle my shoe;

Three, four, Shut the door;

Seven, eight, Lay them straight;

Write the correct sequence here: 3 4 1 5 2

Sequencing

Try this rhyme too...
The sequence of the given rhyme is jumbled up. Write the correct sequence in the boxes below.

Read and enjoy the rhyme

Where is Thumbkin? Where is Thumbkin?
Here I am! Here I am!
How are you this morning?
Very well, I thank you.
Run away. Run away.

Where is Pointer? Where is Pointer?
Here I am! Here I am!
How are you this morning?
Very well, I thank you.
Run away. Run away.

Where is Middleman? Where is Middleman?
Here I am! Here I am!
How are you this morning?
Very well, I thank you.
Run away. Run away.

Where is Ringman? Where is Ringman?
Here I am! Here I am!
How are you this morning?
Very well, I thank you.
Run away. Run away.

Where is Pinkie? Where is Pinkie?
Here I am! Here I am!
How are you this morning?
Very well, I thank you.
Run away. Run away.

Where is Ringman? Where is Ringman?
Here I am! Here I am!
How are you this morning?
Very well, I thank you.
Run away. Run away.

Where is Middleman? Where is Middleman?
Here I am! Here I am!
How are you this morning?
Very well, I thank you.
Run away. Run away.

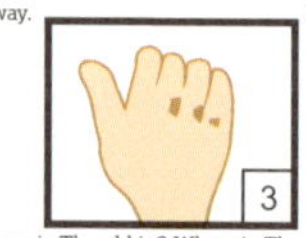

Where is Thumbkin? Where is Thumbkin?
Here I am! Here I am!
How are you this morning?
Very well, I thank you.
Run away. Run away.

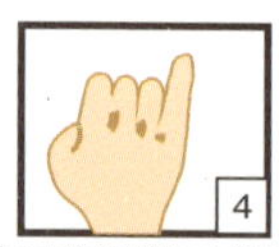

Where is Pinkie? Where is Pinkie?
Here I am! Here I am!
How are you this morning?
Very well, I thank you.
Run away. Run away.

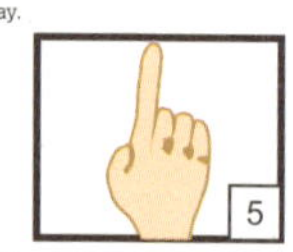

Where is Pointer? Where is Pointer?
Here I am! Here I am!
How are you this morning?
Very well, I thank you.
Run away. Run away.

Write the correct sequence here: 3 5 2 1 4

Answer key

Algorithm

Choose and place the correct arrows in the grid to make the monkey reach the bananas.

↓	→	←	↑

Draw the correct algorithm here:

→	→	↓

Algorithm

Look at these algorithm sets. Which one will you use to help the mouse reach the cheese? Tick the correct one and draw the arrows in the grid below.

Algorithm set 1	Algorithm set 2
↓ ↓ →	↓ ↓ ↓ ←

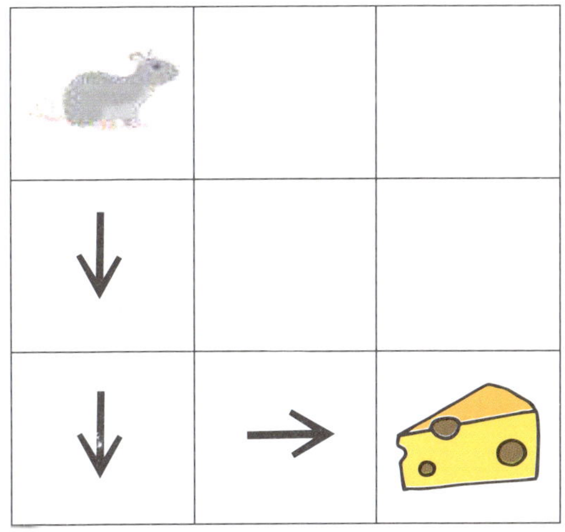

Let's try a debugging activity

Circle the obstacle that made Jack and Jill fall down the hill.

I have started coding with Yash and Yashika

Children learnt the pre-basic coding skills through this storivity (story cum activities) with Yash and Yashika. The various elements of coding are explained simply for a child to understand.

Here are the coding skills that your child learnt in this storivity.

1

I can sequence ...
I learnt to sequence through number and finger rhymes and also activities involving my daily routine.

2

I can spot and create patterns ...
I now understand that pattern is an arrangement of things that repeat in a logical way. Through worksheets and rhymes, I am now able to spot and create patterns.

3

Because I can pattern and sequence, I can now understand algorithms ...
I learnt to give and follow specific instructions in sequential steps.

4

I can debug ...
I learnt to identify errors (bugs) through worksheets and activities.

5

I can loop ...
I understand the concept of looping (repeating again and again) through songs and rhymes.

6

I can use If-Then conditionals ...
If-Then conditionals help me to understand if I have to perform an action or not. This is dependent on whether the statement is true or false. I learnt to use conditionals by playing If-Then-Else board games.

7

I can code ...
I have developed pre-basic set of coding skills like sequencing, patterning, debugging, creating algorithms, looping, using conditionals and am now ready to begin coding robots.

All the activities in the book lay a foundation for children to understand coding. This book enables the young generation to not only be equipped to use technology safely but also learn to code.

About the author

Swati is a born tinkerer! She was a hyperactive child who enjoyed boisterous play and experimenting with objects and gadgets. Now, she designs curriculums that help children tinker and help adults understand how to harness a child's learning capacity. With over three decades of experience as an educator, Swati is on the global think tank team of Kidzania and is the president of Early Childhood Association. She has designed the world's first curriculum for coding for early years and over 45,000 children are presently using it at 500 Podar Jumbo Kids kindergartens! She has included activities like Froebel gifts, readiness games, listening and instruction games and puppetry to help children learn to understand coding as she believes that coding will help children's brains understand how to learn and not just what to learn!